BIG WIN!

A LIFE CHANGING GUIDE

FOR SUCCESFULL GAMBLING

THAT GOES BEYOND SLOTS

TO GIVE YOU AN ECONOMIC PERSPECTIVE

LIKE NO OTHER WITH STORIES,

IDEAS, TIPS AND TRICKS

THAT WILL HELP YOU LIVE AS A WINER

WEY BEYOND SLOTS

Daniel S. M.

BIG
WIN!

First Printing: 2016

ISBN 978-1-365-36125-8

Daniel Sanchez
POST OFFICE BOX 252
AGUADA, PR 00602

CONTENT

1

INTRODUCTION

In a world of infinite ways of
making and expend our money
someone realized that they were
not enough ways of making people
get rid of their money faster and
voluntarily.

Instead of individuals choosing to
buying a business, save, pay of their
debts go for vacations and travel
the world, go to watch a show or a
play or the symphony, go for a hike
a road trip or anything else you
could think of with your money.

Someone invented the slot machine. An entertainment device that certainly entertain us

And now more than ever.

I was thinking and I came up with an easy way to define gambling

Gambling is the volunteer surrender of hard to earn money on the assumption of significantly multiply that money.

This definition well defines the stock market as well. You see constantly on the news how people lose all their saving on bad investment or bad bet and this is not any less risky than gambling.

Since saving have been discourage by taxes and low interests is natural to look for short cut to multiply our money and on that journey the losers will suffer in most cases un reparable damages to say the least.

There is damage cause to the fellow players that hand their money to someone else. Or to yourself by having to pay taxes and big wins if you don't exercise self-control and stop before putting that money back into the system.

Yes, the money you win was someone else's money. But that's just how the system works. And as long as you realize this and how to take advantage of the system you remain a winner.

Gambling still illegal in some states, counties, countries around the world Mainly because poverty is attributed to gambling, plus is prone to addiction ounce you get used to winning or the hope of winning.

I have seen people begging for money on the street and then take that money and instead of buying food they gamble.

Is a fact that the person or entity who owns the casino invest a nice amount of money back to the economy buy building new hotels and businesses and hiring thousands of work force, or expending on a new toy like a luxury car, apartment, and so on. All good examples of what we should do with our money as well.

Unlike some table games as well as the video versions of them that required skills, knowledge of the game, being very smart and good at math. Slot play requires you basically none of the above but you soon realize why you have been a winner already maybe unknowingly.

2

You are a winner!

Your economic situation is in your hand. Gambling is a personal choice.

If You have ever gamble you realize that you have win many times this is not a matter of winning is more about when to stop and saying to gambling enough, sayonara, adieu, good bye, adios, ciao, till next time.

This guide is intended to give you the knowledge to confidentially know when is the best time to play and win.

Wish casinos are most likely to win, wish machines to play.

Most people go to the casino and play make a couple of hundreds and go.

If you don't have the discipline to do so you have to realize

that beneath the amazing architecture of hotels and casinos

nice cocktail waiters and waitresses, colorful hypnotic machines and music from the machines;

You are in a business not a charitable house.

The main goal is to make them money

However, you can be a winner and everyone is but not everyone is willing to go home relax and come back later bud the ambition to make a life changing amount of money doesn't let them quit on time.

When you finish reading you may realize you are actually a winner. If you have been vulnerable of common

mistakes on the presumption that you could hit the big jackpot.

Wish is a possibility certainly

if you err carious about making money you have to have your mind clear.

You can do so by going to the casino well rested

and avoid alcohol at all cost, alcohol is a depressant and kill your inhibitions

if you start drinking your soon forget about the main goal wish is have fun and be a winner

most of the machines start winning.

you have to take the money and leave

if you go to the casino with a one-hundred-dollar budget at no cost withdraw money and continue paling

unless you are extremely wealthy this may not affect you

but the majority of us aren't.

in this book you'll see example of peoples who have win the jackpot in to the millions and are as poor as before in a year and most of the time

highly indebted

this have an easy explanation let me abound

you may have heard that rich people get richer

this is because ounce you have money you realize that is not enough

For example

let's say you win 100,000 you soon realize that may not be enough for paying of your mortgage car and debts

I was in a similar position ounce.

Is all about money management

you can do several things. For example;

Open a bank account that you can't have easy access to the money just so you can set automatic payments of your car house phone bills and credit cards for years to come or you can pay of and cancel small credit card debts and anything else the money last for.

I have done that myself and is well rewarding

living debt free is an amazing sensation

but living both debts free and having some saving is even better

specially for the mental Piz.

But that was not always the case specially when I started using my saving on the hope of making a life changing amount of money then I started looking at my behavior and the behavior of others inside the casino

and was then that I keep seeing that everyone including me am a winner the bells keep making that sound and sirens when they hit a winning combination

and then I look and see a BIG WIN on the screen.

yes, if I have taken the money and come back another day or try in another machine we all live a big winner

But on the hope of winning that big jackpot and hypnotized by the colors and sounds

and margaritas and gin we just keep hitting the repeat bet button

time after time after time till there's no money left.

I still remember and have the clear picture in my mind of this lady

I couldn't understand her well because she has too many drinks already

after playing all the money she has

She then realized she has nothing left to pay for a taxi or even to eat a ship burger from a fast food

At that time, I was in this machine and hit a big win

I won about 300 dollars so I give her 20 dollar for the cab

then I see her again and guess what? yes she uses that money gamble it and yes she didn't win

this is sad to reach that point.

I guaranteed that she won at the beginning but did not quit on time and on the presumption of winning that life changing amount of money couldn't stop

let's do the math here

yes, this is just a mathematical matter controlled by algorithm, computer microchip and even probably AI and who knows what else.

Having a well understanding of how the odds work will increase your chance of winning big

virtual reel decreases the odds significantly.

some of this machines have the jackpot running in the hundred thousand an even million dollars.

most casinos even have a sign on the machines that return the most money to the gambler

may say 98% and even 99% payback

those machines are placed in high traffic areas where celebrating gamblers catch the attention

of people walking by or eating and make them feel they can win as well

so they stop open their wallets and start hoping for their moment

most gamblers prefer to gamble in this machines

even when mathematically the odds should be the same

most of this machines also make you believe that you are almost about to win

so you can keep putting money on them avoid them at all cost

also most of the modern day machines move their reels in a total unpredictable nontraditional way

increasing the odds of winning even more

Believing in secret that the next time you hit that spin button

will be the winning combination may keep you sit for hours

since ounce you get inside the casino any perception of time and space are lost

there's no morning or night bad or good weather

you could easily be stock in a 24-hour infinite loop

So stop

you can come back when you relax again. Use that money to have a nice meal or enjoy a show or a movie.

I have seen this too many times is that the slot start making a few hundreds and then stop winning and if you just sat hoping for more hypnotized unable to realize that today may not be the day you go home with the thousand or million dollar you end up losing it all.

3

The psychological game of slots

Those carefully engineered machines are really amazing

Just walk around and see the creativity involved on those machines the details the music and the effects

You can feel something going on in the back of your brain. Like skydiving or a roller coaster. Adrenaline?

 I can't explain it, perhaps the expectation of what could happen next as you play.

Any slot could potentially be about to release that precious price.

don't get stock in the same machine if you are not winning anything within the first few spins.

Switch to another machine. some machines say that they pay more like the picture in the cover

Those machines are more likely to pay. However, because they pay more often the amount cod be less

than those million number goal. the odds of becoming millionaire from owning your own business are less than the odds of winning multimillion dollar jackpot. In other words, is faster to work that million by owning your own business

Than hoping to strike that winning combination on a slot. that is when you have to stop

If the machine gives you the choice to change the denomination, choose a higher denomination.

This will multiply the amount of money to be paid.

Other machines allow you to stop the reels. I love this one because I stop it when I spot a winning combination

Therefor hitting a win. Most of the time what I'm looking to hit is those free games.

Free games will let you save the money and let the machine giving you instead.

Free games that was my goal when I get them I let the computer do their thing.

I can't contain my excitement every time and that's exactly what the casino wants that's why there is a spared rumor that most of the machines with a larger odd of winning are located in places that unexperienced persons can notice your celebration and attract them to any machine.

The goal is more player to the machine. Remember they don't run a charity, the casino is a business and therefore they are in the business of making money.

Go around the floor of the casino and start looking at those machines.

The first machine was created by a mechanic but today machines by engineers and most likely psychologies

They use words and statements to persuade you.

You may read things like; up to one hundred free games or seven hundred ways of winning

I have sit at machines that seems to hit a winning combination every time distracting you from one reality that is that your money is being absorbed slowly but surely.

They go up and down like a bouncing ball. This machines are okay if what you want is a little distraction and expend some time at the casino floor.

But think about it after hitting hundreds of times and still no jackpot because the odds are in the thousands per one.

Most of the machines doesn't seems to mind to give you small jackpots and rewards every now and then.

Is when we want that big jackpot and keep playing and playing and end up losing everything.

Get used to winning. Winning small or winning large is winning. One day you'll be the next and within those first spins you're going to get that cash that you want.

That way you won't loose and still have that satisfaction of having a good time in a casino.

The one thing that cause people to lose large amounts of money is that they try to recover from that lose.

Some people call that chasing your money and is in that process that people star losing.

Is a wired feeling, like having revenge on the machine that took your money and don't want to give it back.

Try learning to play a skill game there are more people that win in video poker or video card those machines are within the slots

but studying and learning those slot machines will be very rewarding some of those require math knowledge and rules that are explained if you press the game rules or instructions right there on each machine.

As some gambler have told me is better to play those video card games and other more complex slots that the regular slots if your goal is winning. They see the regular slot machines as a quick way of losing the money and avoid them at all cost but they do recognize that free games multipliers and other futures those machines have make them very tempting to play and if you win can be very rewarding.

Whatever machine you choose among many depending on the casino you should find the one you feel comfortable. Then play a few bucks and move one.

Many machines will suck your money right away while other will have a balance of winning and loses

I have seen person playing the same machine for hours perhaps thinking in secret I'm going to win that jackpot.

But are those machines that will give you entertainment and a show that I like the most and at the same time if it happens to win big even better.

Spotting the right machine is relatively easy since most of them will be taken by other people that frequent the casino.

Don't be afraid to ask fellow players because some of them have players' cards and are in the casino on a daily basis they know better, let them share their stories. Look for the casino advertising big wins on specific type of machines.

However, machines that have recently given big jackpots are less likely to do it two times in a row.

Avoid getting hypnotized by the bells and flashing light like Deers and cobras. And don't lose the focus. Don't get out of budget and live with positive number, with a profit.

Above all keep it fun and quit when stop being funny.

4

When you win the million

I started a curiosity to know about how people live after winning big jackpots and lotteries.

On my research I found that most of those people are broke.

That without mentioning sport players and people that inherit a large amount of money somehow that end up broke for the same reasons explained below.

Their case is even worse than before. Sure they may have memories of all they did with their money.

But think about it, do you need a 5000-dollar purse? that amount of money is about five months of salary for the average minimum wage workers so why waste that amount of money that could potentially help you and your family live worriless for years to come.

There are full documentaries available over the internet about this subject. You'll be amazed. And learning about it before hand is very important. Learning from someone else mistakes is the ideal because there are plenty of examples to follow.

I previously mention about how gambling is not as different as the stock market.

Well, most of those people lost their money in bad investments from the stock market and other types of investments.

Additionally, the influence of fake friendship and family members and all sort of advisors who want to control and somehow all of the sudden they think what is best to do with your money.

Try to keep your money yours and avoid the desperation to multiply those millions of dollars and try to become even more wealthy.

This obsession causes them not only to lose all of their money but to be even indebted.

Having that amount of money gives you plenty of time to go and take a course on how to be a business owner and how to invest not just believe what someone else tells you.

I was ounce victim of fraud from a company that seems to be totally legitimate.

I still have the card to withdraw money and make transactions and letters and emails. Below this apparent stable company, the investment firm end up being a fraud and I lot it all.

I talk about this company to my brother and he was interested on participating as is natural to anybody.

But I remember saying let me do it first just in case turn up to be a scam.

That way I avoided losing my and someone else money.

There are so many cases just as the one I experience.

A quick search on the internet and you'll be flooded of stories like that one.

That's the way of life of scammers and fraudulent companies to try to take advantage

Then they make you sing disclosures Legal forms that say this transaction is not guaranteed and that you may lose your money.

When instead should say that losing your investment is guaranteed.

Have you ever look at those people salaries and bonuses? and what about the fees they charge on your investment?

Is sad that this still exist we will be a much richer country if the worker's money remains in their pockets.

Ounce you have some savings the priority should be to save as much as you can to keep you living worriless.

The world environment is in constant change and thing happens that affect the cash flow and with a nice number of savings you can afford to continue living your life unaffected.

To get the picture look at Greece, Argentina, Venezuela, Spain and many more countries whose economy have collapse at some point.

is that proverbial ant who work and save that suffer the least.

5

What about taxes

Taxes are a big issue when winning jackpots over the one thousand mark

Depending of the game played, some starting points to report large amounts of taxes may vary.

I even notice that the machine asks to call the attendant to pay.

Most machines even stop allowing you play till they get your information fill the appropriate tax form and you get paid. And then you get a form over the mail so you can share a big chunk of that amount with the government.

I know of someone that stop playing after having to pay thousands of dollars in taxes.

Especially when they have to pay whether or not they put that money back into the system by continuing playing

Forgetting to live with the profit.

The amount to pay is 31% in taxes to the government.

Basically you are winning jackpots on behalf of the IRS

That why I care about smaller pays than big wins. Big wins in the long run will cost me big as well.

_____

Smaller wins after smaller wins will pile up over time.

As well as smaller loses after smaller loses.

The good news is Gambling losses are deductible.

Ask the casino how can you have proof of how much money you put on gambling so you can deduct that amount.

Usually by using a players' card not only you can track how much money you win or lose also they give you point and prizes.

I talk to a teller and they even send you a yearly report that can be used as a proof of how much money you have put into the system versus how much you have win when filing the taxes that way the fun continues without being unpleasantly surprised even may end up paying nothing.

If you are going to expend that money anyway will be better to track down how much have you put in to the system and take advantage of this expense.

RESPONSIBLE GAMING MEANS:
Knowing when to stop
WHO WE ARE
CAESARS CODE OF COMMITMENT

6

When having fun stop being funny

Knowing when to stop

When the fun stop

This are the titles of some brochures around Las Vegas casinos.

They realize that falling into an addictive and irresponsible behavior is easy.

And cause many damages to you and whoever cares about you.

Some people think that gambling should be reserved to multimillionaires that such a life style won't create such a big whole in their pocket or largely affect them.

For the rest of us loosing what we earn is a big deal

Especially if someone else depend of your salary, or have debts car payments or just need the money to live with dignity and go to restaurant and have fun.

Gambling is just one example of a way to lose the money, there are many addictions that will take money out of what should be essential and we should not blame the game solely.

When you exercise self-control you can translate that to other aspects of your life and became a better person overall.

Is when you lie to yourself saying I will bet this amount and just keep hoping to win that amount of

money that will change your life that you end up losing the money you need to cover essential expenses.

Those pamphlets are designed for people that realize they need help

Forums, gamblers anonymous, groups are some examples of possible help you may find as a result of calling. Visiting a psychology, psychiatrist and social worker should help very good as well,

However, this programs are available for free so there's no expenses involved. By using this programs.

If you go to a local church or group or club openly talk about what is happening. Soon you'll find that you are not the only one.

Most people don't Voluntarily tend to talk about their weaknesses and flaws. But are willing to do so ounce you start opening up.

However, in the process is normal to find people that will judge you.

Don't be afraid to say don't judge me, because even when some people don't confess or talk about what they do wrong they certainly have hidden stories that can be worse than yours

That's why this groups exist. by sharing each other stories you get back in track.

If that's the case.

7

Over confidence, outcome and expectations

let's talk about over confidence and outcome

you may have notice multiple times about my emphasis on saving money

some economist suggests having at least six months' worth of savings to covet recurring expenses

this have not always been my point of view

and I wish I have lean this in advance and no by my self

and those where painful and sad moments of my life

that I wish I'm able to transmit to you how important this is

let me tell you a story about what happened to me

At one point of my life I was able to save enough money to live comfortably for about two years

however, I was confident of two things one I will find a job quick enough and

be able to recover the savings

and second that I may be able to win a huge jackpot that will change my life even when i was winning small amount of money on the machines those did not compensate my overall expenses

and my savings where quickly exploited till I started getting in to panic mode from the possibility of not finding a job or a source of income that can cover my expenses.

I was living my life like I was rich and that the money will las forever.

Even when I was debt free I fail by being over confident and getting a different outcome that what I have planned in my imagination.

I fail by thinking future money was more important that what I currently have in savings.

I still need money to eat, pay my car insurance, Gas, cell phone and any other expense that may occur

those monthly payments will look big if there is not enough money to cover them.

It was appropriate for me to correct this behavior as soon as possible.

At the end I end up finding multiple sources of income as was advised on a book I read

call "Income without a job". plus, I found two other jobs.

it was completely unnecessary to do this if I only was able to control my expenses and make that money last as much as possible.

By keeping expectation realistic all the deception will be made by reason and no by instinct

If you decided to invest your saving, make sure the principal is guaranteed or that they have an insurance policy

That way the savings will stay intact in case the expected growth doesn't happens or loss of value

If you are unemployed set a maximum of money allow to cover the necessities and stay within the budget.

Till the cash flow are restituted.

Piz of mind is of much more value

will save you from unnecessary stress and wariness

And specially from having a job you don't enjoy just because of the need for money.

_____

8

Save! Save! Save!

Saving is not quitting on spending.

A recession is seen as a bad thing Responsible expending is good for You unlike just buying impulsively and then have too much of everything.

At one point of my life I use to have a lot of collections that end up being eaten by termite humidity, stolen or damaged.

I end up selling what was left and since then I have the least amount of stuff possible.

I also remember when moving out of my house. When I move out of my second apartment after four years I have so much that I have to make so many trips to finally move.

So I say never again and from that point on I started having less every day and my cash saving start going up.

Being a savers save the economy in many ways during a recession cause by any reason. Savers slowly use their money in the normal expenses or to cover bills.

In 2008 our economic system suffers greatly with the burst of the housing bubble, almost all financial institution suffers.

think about what would happened if every person has one or two years' worth of savings accumulated. Probably no back would need a bailout.

The collapse was cause mainly Because suddenly people lose their jobs and weren't able to pay their mortgages and other expenses.

If all of them where savers they could still make payments and the system could continue working

and will give savers plenty of time to find a job and resume their life normally

The consequences of not saving something at least a month so we can adapt to changes.

When I use to have a minimum wage job it was difficult for me to save. But thinking back was till my fault in part. Sometimes my income was less than expected and I move to a least expensive apartment or cell phone plan.

Saving money is like the hoover dam, save the water and slowly release it as need it

They can make electricity out of it or for consumption in cities

Even saving that amount of water won't take of their mind the possibility of one day running out of water if those savings don't replenish fast enough

That have been the topic of multiple documentaries

With the dam example you realize that by saving is possible to make a smart use of the resources we have than just letting all go.

The exact same thing happens to us being a saver mean to make use of our money slowly and efficiently.

9

Conclusion

Grab any denomination dollar bill in your hand or imagine you have one

Now think you are right in front of the machine just inserting bills

seeing how the slot machine get that money that most of us earn the hard way and ask yourself why to play at all?

This also is true with online purchases and credit cards

There are many articles on people addicted to online purchases unlike online purchases that people can return or resell the item to recover the money that's not possible on gambling. Unless you have a way to document and deduct from the taxes.

Casinos and slot machines are a good source of entertainment with touch screen, motion, sound and 3d effects.

Now more than ever they are more sophisticated with lots of way of keeping us distracted and with the hope alive of wining that live changing amount of money while doing so.

but don't lose yourself. Have in mind that is easy to get out of budget and regret it for years to come. Get use to win a little and go home. One day will be your turn to win it big

Win friends and met people in the process learn from the experience wish machine or casino is best for you, take advantage of the points and benefits casino have to offer

remember that any loss you have is deductible as long as you have proof

save and retain enough money to have a Piz of mind to keep doing what you love.

Ask for help if necessary to go back on track.

avoid to fall in any new addiction like smoking or drinking that could be easier in that environment

For me winning the slots go beyond the cash rewards. Is More entertainment.

Yes, leaving ounce I win most of the time takes courage.

sometimes wanting to win more and large amount of money can keep me playing till I lose more than what can I afford to lose.

Winning over the slots also mean for me resign at the possibility of easy money, and other times means going and have lots of fun and enjoy this pieces of engineering.

But always with self-control while keeping within the budget.

Winning Big most of the time means for me having the strength of not going to play at all

and avoid expending that money that I need to live my life with dignity and out of poverty.

That's a big win!

www.ingramcontent.com/pod-product-compliance
Lightning Source LLC
Chambersburg PA
CBHW022130170526
45157CB00004B/1820